QUESTIONING HISTORY

The Causes of World War II

Stewart Ross

HODDER
Wayland

an imprint of Hodder Children's Books

© 2003 White-Thomson Publishing Ltd

Produced for Hodder Wayland by
White-Thomson Publishing Ltd
2/3 St Andrew's Place
Lewes BN7 1UP

Other titles in this series:
The African-American Slave Trade
The Cold War
The Holocaust
The Western Front

Editor: Cath Senker
Designer: Derek Lee
Consultant: Terry Charman
Picture research: Shelley Noronha and
Cath Senker, Glass Onion Pictures
Proofreader: Philippa Smith

Published in Great Britain in 2003 by Hodder
Wayland, an imprint of Hodder Children's Books

British Library Cataloguing in Publication Data
Ross, Stewart
  Causes of World War II (Questioning history)
  1. World War (1939–1945) – Causes - Juvenile
  literature
  I. Title II. Senker, Cath
  940.5'3'11

ISBN 0 7502 4082 2

Printed in Hong Kong

Hodder Children's Books
A division of Hodder Headline Limited
338 Euston Road, London NW1 3BH

Picture acknowledgements:
AKG *cover, title page,* 11, 14, 21, 34, 42; AKG
London 8, 10, 15, 19, 22, 26, 31, 35, 36, 37, 40,
44, 45, 58, 59; Camera Press 32; Hodder Wayland
Picture Library 22, 23, (Imperial War Museum)
27, (IWM) 41, (IWM) 43, 47, (IWM) 48,
(IWM) 49, (IWM) 50, (IWM) 55, (IWM) 57,
60, (IWM) 61; Peter Newark 18, 33, 38, 51, 53,
54; Popperfoto 5, 6, 7, 17, 25, 28, 29, 30, 46;
Topham Picturepoint 12, 39; TRH Pictures 24,
(National Archive) 56.

The maps on pages 4 and 9 were produced by
The Map Studio.

Cover picture: Hitler driving in an open car
through Brno during the Nazi take-over of
Czechoslovakia in March 1939.

CONTENTS

CHAPTER 1

From One War to Another

The Second World War did not begin on a particular day. It was made up of various conflicts in different places, each starting at a different time. Gradually, as more countries became involved, people began to speak of a world war.

THREE WARS

There were three main areas of conflict: Europe, the Far East and the Pacific Ocean. Other campaigns were fought in North Africa, the Caucasus (east of the Black Sea) and South-east Asia. Fighting took place on the ground, in the skies and across the world's oceans.

The war in the Far East began in 1937, when Japan began a full-scale attack on China. The European war started in 1939 with Nazi Germany's invasion of Poland. The Nazi attack on the Soviet Union, starting in June 1941, dramatically expanded the European war. The Western and Eastern wars came together in

LEFT *German expansion, 1939–41.* RIGHT *The Japanese advance, 1941–2.*

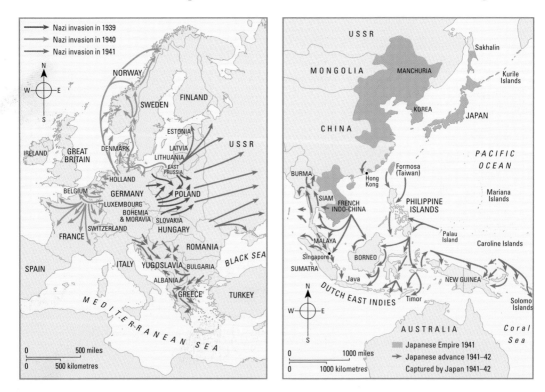

4

December 1941, when Japan attacked the American naval base of Pearl Harbor. This, coupled with attacks on British colonies by the Japanese, forced the USA and the British Empire into war with Japan. Days afterwards, Germany went to war with the USA. By the end of 1941, therefore, we can talk of a truly world war.

A TROUBLED WORLD

Obviously, these conflicts did not all break out for the same reasons. This makes it difficult to generalize about why the Second World War started. Nevertheless, there are certain links between the different outbreaks of fighting. The war occurred in a deeply troubled world. Many of the roots of that trouble can be traced back twenty years, to the end of the last great conflict: the First World War (1914–18).

BELOW *The representatives of the Allies by the railway carriage where they signed the Armistice.*

? EVENT IN QUESTION

Armistice, 1918: defeat or stab in the back?

World War I ended when the Germans and the Allies, led by France, Britain and the USA, signed an armistice (cease-fire) agreement on 11 November 1918. The Allies were represented by their commander-in-chief, Marshal Ferdinand Foch, and the Germans by Matthias Erzberger and other politicians. One of the problems that haunted the post-war world was why this Armistice had been signed.

Foch and Erzberger said Germany had been defeated. The German people were in revolt. Their allies – Turkey, Bulgaria and Austria-Hungary – had already surrendered. The navy had mutinied and the army was in retreat.

Later, Adolf Hitler and the Nazis insisted that Germany had not been defeated. Instead, they said, its army had been 'stabbed in the back' (betrayed) by politicians, trade unionists and Jews as it withdrew towards Germany.

The First World War

When World War I ended, most world leaders were determined nothing causing destruction on such a huge scale should ever happen again. The war, they said, had been 'the war to end all wars'.

A Lost Generation

The war had caused dreadful loss of life: 1.8 million German soldiers, 1.7 million Russians, 1.4 million French, 1.2 million Austro-Hungarians, 0.9 million from the British Empire. Together with the hundreds of thousands from other nations, the total figure of military dead may have been 13 million. The number injured was perhaps three times that figure. Civilian deaths and injuries also ran into millions.

BELOW *British soldiers wounded at the Battle of the Somme (1916), some of the millions of casualties of the First World War.*

Most of those killed or wounded were young men aged 18 to 30. Many were volunteers – the best of their generation, eager to do the right thing for their country. So many natural leaders had been killed that Winston Churchill described Britain's post-war government as a 'Second XI'.

The war had also brought about massive destruction. Large areas of France and Russia had become desolate wastelands. The German, Austro-Hungarian, Russian and Turkish Empires had collapsed. Russia was in the hands of communists who threatened to carry their revolution across the rest of Europe and beyond.

Of the major wartime powers, only Japan and the USA did not suffer greatly. This was significant. Although they had fought a short war with Russia in 1904–5, few Japanese people had first-hand experience of the horrors of modern warfare. US battle casualties were also low.

PUNISHMENT

The task of seeing that the miseries of 1914–18 were not repeated rested with the victors – principally France, Britain and the USA. They had a choice: forget the past and build a more tolerant future, or start by punishing those they believed responsible for the war. In choosing the latter, they took the first step towards a Second World War.

RIGHT *US President Woodrow Wilson (left) at the Versailles Peace Conference, 1919. French Prime Minister Georges Clemenceau is walking beside him.*

? PEOPLE IN QUESTION

President Woodrow Wilson (1856–1924)

After the war, Wilson believed the USA should help to build a better world on the ruins of the old. In January 1918 he set out his vision in Fourteen Points. One of his central ideas – peace without blame – was rejected by the Versailles Peace Conference of 1919 (see page 8). The US Senate rejected a second key concept, a League of Nations to preserve peace and resolve international conflict (see page 12). This left the League to manage as best it could without the world's most powerful nation. If fellow politicians had listened to US president Woodrow Wilson in 1918, might a Second World War have been avoided?

7

ABOVE *Negotiators at Brest-Litovsk, where Germany forced Russia to accept humiliating peace terms.*

MAKING PEACE

Several peace treaties followed the First World War. In March 1918, just before the war ended, Germany forced Russia to sign the Treaty of Brest-Litovsk. Its terms, extremely favourable to the Germans, were later overturned at Versailles. The Treaties of Saint-Germain (1919) and Trianon (1920) arranged the break-up of the Austro-Hungarian Empire. Because the empire had largely collapsed before the war ended, these treaties were not seen to be particularly controversial.

The Treaty of Neuilly (1919, negotiated at Versailles) took lands from Bulgaria. Turkey's future, also discussed at Versailles, was set out in the Treaty of Sèvres (1920). These treaties caused resentment but not sufficient to threaten another major war.

VERSAILLES

Germany's future was dictated by the Treaty of Versailles (1919), which it had no choice but to accept. It lost territory to France, Denmark, Belgium, Poland and Lithuania. Danzig, the Saar region and Germany's overseas colonies were put under the control of the League of Nations (see page 12). German armaments were limited: for example, Germany was not allowed an air force and was permitted to have an army of only 100,000 soldiers after a wartime strength of around four million men.

REPARATIONS

The Germans were particularly humiliated by a clause that blamed them for the war and obliged them to pay reparations (compensation) for the damage they had caused. In 1921 this was fixed at an impossible 132 billion gold marks (£6,600 million).

Some observers realized that the treaty's harsh terms might not be the best way to preserve peace. Marshal Foch, for example, correctly predicted that it would be only a 'twenty-year cease-fire'. This was by no means inevitable: much depended on how well the new world order settled down.

> ### ? WHAT IF...
>
> ### the victors had been less harsh on Germany?
>
> The leaders of the Allied countries – France, Britain, the USA and Italy – did not agree on how Germany should be treated after the war. The French, who had suffered most, wanted harsher terms than the Americans and the British. The task of British and French politicians was made harder by public demands for Germany to be 'squeezed like a lemon'.
>
> Early in 1918 US President Wilson had suggested 'Fourteen Points' for future peace. They did not mention war guilt or reparation payments. The Germans claimed they had signed the Armistice on the basis of the Fourteen Points, so Versailles had cheated them. If the Treaty had been less harsh, might the Germans have felt less resentful?

BELOW *Europe after the First World War.*

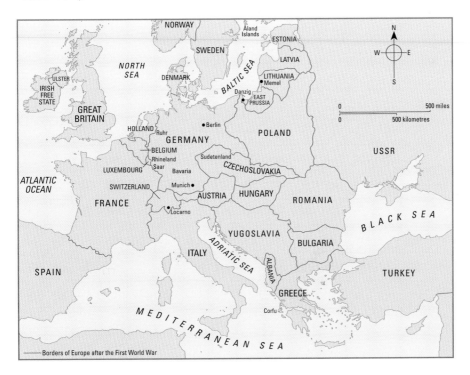

Borders of Europe after the First World War

THE SOVIET UNION

After the Treaty of Versailles, two countries were a source of potential conflict in Europe: Germany and communist Russia (from 1922 called the Soviet Union, or the USSR). When Russia's civil war ended in 1922, Vladimir Lenin, the Soviet leader, rejected further warfare.

After Lenin's death in 1924, power gradually passed to Joseph Stalin, who was content to develop communism within the Soviet Union. By 1928 there was no immediate threat of a war between western Europe and the USSR.

THE WEIMAR REPUBLIC

After 1919, Germany had a new democratic government, called the Weimar Republic. It struggled to survive. In January 1919 the Republic was threatened by communists, who seized Berlin and other German cities during the Spartacist Rising. The government defeated them, helped by anti-communist ex-soldiers – the *Freikorps*.

The right-wing *Freikorps* also threatened the Weimar Republic. Its members despised democracy and believed the politicians had betrayed them in 1918. However, following the

BELOW *Armed Spartacists (communists) in the streets of Berlin where they tried unsuccessfully to start a revolution.*

LES ALEMANDS OBSERVENT LES 2 MINUTES DE SILENCE.

LEFT *Germans holding a two-minute silence in protest at France's occupation of the Ruhr industrial region in 1923.*

Freikorps' failed coup, the Kapp Putsch of March 1920, the threat from right-wing groups began to fade. It flared again briefly in November 1923, when Adolf Hitler tried to seize the government of Bavaria in the Beer Hall Putsch.

INFLATION AND RECOVERY

At first the Weimar Republic had serious economic problems. Almost bankrupt, Germany could not meet its reparation payments. The French and Belgians responded in January 1923 by temporarily occupying the Ruhr, Germany's main industrial area. They took goods such as coal and iron in place of money. This led to the total collapse of the value of the German currency, the mark, and roaring inflation. By late 1923 there were 4.2 million marks to US$1. People went shopping carrying suitcases stuffed with banknotes.

From 1924 onwards the situation in Germany began to improve. Inflation was controlled and reparations were reduced. Employment increased, civil violence fell away and prosperity began to return. By 1928 many Germans viewed the future with cautious optimism.

? EVENT IN QUESTION

French occupation of the Ruhr, 1923–4: justified?

When French and Belgian troops entered the Ruhr area in January 1923, German workers went on strike. The Ruhr ground to a halt and the French collected only a fraction of what they wanted.

The French government said the occupation was necessary to uphold the Treaty of Versailles and ensure that France received justice. After all, when defeated by Germany in 1871, France had paid reparations to Germany.

The Weimar Republic's politicians argued that the occupation only made matters worse. It slowed German economic recovery, making it harder to pay reparations. It also stirred old Franco-German hatred, making a lasting peace less likely.

Salle des Assemblées

Salle du Conseil

Secrétariat

ABOVE *Symbol of hope for a better world: the League of Nations headquarters in Geneva, Switzerland.*

THE LEAGUE OF NATIONS

The Treaty of Versailles set up the League of Nations, an organization that was supposed to represent all the countries of the world. Its principal aim was 'collective security' – all nations were to act together to keep world peace. The League was established to settle international disputes and promote international understanding. Germany was not invited to join. The US Senate, on the other hand, voted not to. It wanted the USA to be free of international commitments, a policy called isolationism.

The League of Nations was based in Geneva, Switzerland. It operated through a General Assembly, representing all members, and a smaller Council of more powerful nations, such as Britain and France.

THE LEAGUE'S ACHIEVEMENTS

Some disputes were settled (for example, a dispute between Finland and Sweden over the Baltic's Åland Islands in 1920) when both sides accepted the League's decision. In theory, if one side rejected the League's judgement, the principle of 'collective security' took over. Members banded together to force that nation to mend its ways. They could do this by economic sanctions or, ultimately, by force. Such a decision had to be agreed by all members before it could be carried out.

THE LEAGUE DISCREDITED

Because the League of Nations had no troops of its own, it relied upon its members to provide its 'teeth'. This they refused to do. In other words, if a country defied the League, little or nothing could be done about it. The Italian dictator Benito Mussolini showed this in 1923 (see panel) and 1935, when he conquered Abysinnia (see page 28). So did the Japanese when they invaded Manchuria in 1931 (see page 24).

The League was discredited by its powerlessness. The fact that major countries – the USA, Germany (until 1926) and the Soviet Union (until 1934) – were not members did not help either. It remained a wonderful idea, but unfortunately it proved unable to stop a future war.

? EVENT IN QUESTION

Mussolini's seizure of Corfu, 1923: the League's lost opportunity?

The first time the League of Nations was challenged, it failed to act decisively against aggression. In August 1923, Mussolini used the murder of some Italian military personnel on the Greek island of Corfu as an excuse to capture the island. Although this was just the sort of aggression between member states that the League was designed to stop, it failed to act swiftly or decisively against Italy. In the end, Greece paid Mussolini compensation and he withdrew his forces. The message to the world was clear: aggression could still triumph. Had the League lost a golden opportunity to show its strength?

Gustav Stresemann (1878–1929)

Many Europeans felt that Stresemann's death at the age of 51 was a tragedy for Germany. He was an experienced political leader, respected in France and widely admired elsewhere. Some politicians, such as Winston Churchill, believed that had he lived, he might have guided his country down more moderate paths.

Yet Stresemann was an essential part of the Weimar Republic. The Great Depression discredited the governments of just about every nation. It is likely that the Depression would have ruined Stresemann's career just as it ruined those of other Weimar leaders.

ABOVE *The lost leader: Gustav Stresemann, Germany's foreign minister 1923–9. His early death deprived his country of a fine statesman.*

AN ERA OF PEACE?

Looking back, we might judge that the Treaty of Versailles was unwisely harsh and the League of Nations ill-equipped to keep world peace. Yet neither of these factors made another war likely. As noted, by 1926 the post-war world looked set for a long era of peace.

The most optimistic sign was that hatred between France and Germany was starting to die down. A key figure was Gustav Stresemann, the German foreign minister from 1923 to 1929. He worked tirelessly to improve relations between Germany and its former enemies.

THE SPIRIT OF LOCARNO

In 1925 Germany, France, Britain, Italy and Belgium signed a series of treaties at Locarno, Switzerland that settled many of western Europe's disputed frontiers. The agreements were greeted with popular approval. The following year Germany was admitted to the League of Nations. Regular meetings between the German and French foreign ministers kept the 'spirit of Locarno' alive until Stresemann's death in 1929.

Stresemann also set up the negotiations that produced the Dawes Plan (1924). Arranged by senior US politician Charles Dawes, the plan allowed Germany to pay reparations only when it could afford to. This took a huge strain off the German economy. Later, the Young Plan (1929) drastically cut reparations and extended the time over which they had to be paid.

ARMS LIMITATIONS

Elsewhere the mood was also optimistic. At a conference held in Washington in 1921–2 it was agreed the major powers would limit the size of their navies. In 1928 France and the USA signed the Kellogg-Briand Pact, which rejected war as a way of achieving political aims. Eventually, sixty-three other nations signed the pact. Yet there was no threat of force to back up the agreement.

In 1932 a World Disarmament Conference met in Geneva, Switzerland. It aimed to cut world armaments, something agreed by all League of Nations members. By this time, however, the international mood had darkened and the conference ended in failure.

BELOW *For those with well-paid jobs in the USA and Europe, such as the people here going to the theatre in New York in 1928, the 1920s were a time of high spending and luxurious living.*

CHAPTER 2

Depression

The optimism of the later 1920s disguised deep-seated worries. Democracy was still under threat from both extreme left and right. With prosperity increasing, it was unlikely that people outside the USSR would turn to communism. If the economic situation started to get worse, however, communism might become more popular – just as it had in Russia in 1917.

FASCISM

Like the communists, after World War I the right wing had also enjoyed some success. In 1921 Benito Mussolini had founded the National Fascist Party in Italy. It stood for fierce nationalism, strong leadership in a one-party state and hatred of the left.

In 1922 King Victor Emmanuel III appointed Mussolini prime minister. He made it clear he would govern as a dictator. Mussolini established himself as the leader of a totalitarian fascist state. Fascism ended Italy's political chaos and a big programme of public works was begun. But there was a cost: the end of free speech, opposition parties and trade unions.

? PEOPLE IN QUESTION

Benito Mussolini (1883–1945)

Mussolini said he was bringing the Italian people freedom. He said:

'Fascism stands for liberty and for the only liberty worth having, the liberty of the State and of the individual within the State.' (Doctrine of Fascism, Rome 1932.)

The historian J.M. Roberts takes another view:

'Terror had been a part of Fascism from the start at a local level. In 1923, the 'squads' (fascist groups] were turned into a militia [trained military group] which gave the new regime its own armed force and made it independent of the army. In 1924 violence was carried into parliament, when a socialist deputy, Matteotti, was murdered…'

(*Europe 1880–1945*, Longman, 1982, p.431.)

Could there really be liberty in Mussolini's Italy if citizens did not have the right to criticize the government?

LACK OF ENFORCEMENT

The international agreements of the 1920s depended on governments' goodwill. At the 1921–2 Washington conference, for instance, powers agreed not to seize Chinese territory. But there was no means of policing this pact. Japan, the leading military power in the Far East, was sorely tempted to take advantage of China's weakness.

At Locarno Germany made no guarantee always to accept its new frontiers with Czechoslovakia and Poland. As many German-speakers lived in both countries, the situation was uneasy. Moreover, there was no means of enforcing the Kellogg-Briand Pact to stop war. The League of Nations had serious weaknesses, not least being the absence of both the Soviet Union and the USA.

What Europe really needed was a long period of prosperity in which to settle down. Tragically, in 1929 the optimistic mood of the later 1920s was brought to a sudden, shuddering halt.

The New York Times.

NEW YORK, WEDNESDAY, OCTOBER 30, 1929.

STOCKS COLLAPSE IN 16,410,030-SHARE DAY,
BUT RALLY AT CLOSE CHEERS BROKERS;
BANKERS OPTIMISTIC, TO CONTINUE AID

ABOVE *The headline in The New York Times on 30 October 1929 was optimistic. Yet the collapse of the US stock market was followed by years of deep world-wide economic depression.*

THE GREAT DEPRESSION

The Great Depression was the turning point of the inter-war years. This massive and long-lasting economic collapse started in the USA and spread right across the world. The hardship and misery that it brought had political consequences that led directly to aggression and war.

The Depression was triggered by a dramatic fall in the value of shares on Wall Street, the US stock market, in October 1929. In a matter of days 9 million Americans lost most of their savings. Many lost everything. Thousands of individuals and businesses went bankrupt.

Other stock markets around the world collapsed too. American imports plummeted as the market shrank. This affected producers and manufacturers worldwide. Desperately short of money, Americans also took back huge sums of money loaned to countries such as Germany and Britain.

Between 1929 and the end of 1933 the US economy, the engine of the world economy, shrank by 50 per cent. Over the same period worldwide industrial production fell by 40 per cent.

A WORLD CRISIS

As businesses closed or sacked part of their workforce, unemployment throughout the Western world rose sharply.

In the USA it reached 30 per cent. In Germany it was 33 per cent, with another third not in full-time work. Unemployment led to poverty, loss of self-esteem and anger.

Faced with a totally new situation, governments did not know what to do. For a while it looked as if the entire Western system of democracy and capitalism was cracking up. The older and more stable democracies, such as Britain and the USA, withstood the shock. Elsewhere democracy was threatened from both the left (communism) and right (fascism). In Germany this three-way battle – democracy versus communism versus fascism – was fiercely contested.

? WHAT IF...

the Great Depression had never occurred?

Most historians see a clear link between economic downturn and political upheaval. There were food shortages and rising prices before the French Revolution of 1789 and the Russian Revolution of 1917. Similarly, economic misery and discontent allowed the two major fascist leaders, Mussolini and Hitler, to gain power.

By 1928 Hitler's Nazi Party was little more than a sideshow in German politics. The Depression created the conditions under which it was able to become a major force (see page 20). Hitler's rise to power was a crucial step towards the European war in 1939. One could argue, therefore, that if there had been no Depression, Hitler might never have come to power and there might not have been a Second World War.

LEFT *The American dream turned nightmare? The Great Depression forced millions into the sort of poverty endured by this farming family in Tengle, Alabama.*

19

Rising Aggression

For Germans the democracy of the Weimar Republic was something new after the pre-war German Empire. Extreme right-wingers such as Hitler and ex-general Erich Ludendorff condemned it as un-German. Instead, they wanted the firm and ruthless leadership of a single man. This *Führer* would head an all-powerful fatherland embracing all Germans – the world's master race.

Nazi Revival

In 1928 the Nazis' racist policies were unpopular. Their leader, Hitler, had even spent time in prison in 1923–4 for his part in the Beer Hall Putsch. The Nazis and their far-right supporters had won 32 seats out of 472 in the May 1924 Reichstag (parliamentary) elections but only 12 seats in 1928. Then came the Depression, and everything changed.

As German unemployment rose (1.5 million in mid-1929 to over 6 million by March 1932), so did the appeal of the Nazis. They said that Germany's troubles were caused by an international Jewish conspiracy over which the German master race would triumph. To those who had nothing these ideas explained the present and gave hope for the future. Others looked to communism to solve their problems.

? WHAT IF...

the Nazis' opponents had combined to keep Hitler out of power?

In Weimar Germany the number of seats a party had in the Reichstag was in proportion to the number of votes it received – a system of proportional representation. This gave seats to small parties and made it almost impossible for one party to have total control. Governments were formed from coalitions (alliances) of politicians from different parties.

After the November 1932 elections, left-wing parties had over 221 seats (out of 584) compared with the Nazis' 196. Had they formed an anti-Nazi coalition with, say, the Centre Party (70 seats), Hitler could not have become chancellor and the history of the world might have turned out to be very different.

HITLER COMES TO POWER

The 1930 elections gave the Nazis 107 seats (out of 577) and the communists 77. Two years later (July 1932) the Nazis became the largest party, with 230 seats, and the communists lagged behind with 89. The Nazis still did not have a majority and in November 1932 they won only 196 seats. The communists took 100.

ADOLF – DER ÜBERMENSCH

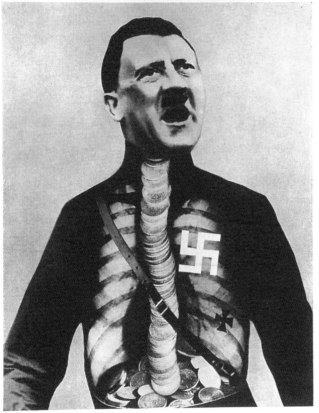

SCHLUCKT GOLD UND REDET BLECH

LEFT *This photomontage created by John Heartfield is anti-Nazi propaganda. It reads 'Hitler, the Superman, swallows gold and talks rubbish.' This shows how Hitler was backed by big business – hence the gold he has swallowed.*

The popularity of the extreme right and extreme left terrified democratic politicians. Leading politicians, including Franz von Papen and Kurt von Schleicher, feared communism more than Nazism. They believed they could control Hitler by giving him office. In January 1933 they persuaded President Hindenburg to appoint Hitler chancellor (prime minister) of Germany. Now he had power, Hitler was determined never to release it.

RIGHT *Nazi propaganda, 1933. The front page of this pamphlet clearly blames the burning of the German Reichstag (parliament) building on the communists.*

Communism in Germany!

The Truth about the Communist Conspiracy on the Eve of the National Revolution

MEIN KAMPF

The appointment of Hitler as German chancellor proved an important step towards war. The threat he posed was obvious. In his book *Mein Kampf* ('My Struggle', first published 1925) he had dismissed the Treaty of Versailles and dreamed of uniting all Germans within a vast new *Reich* (state). He poured scorn on Jews and Slavs, who he believed were 'lesser' races. If he followed such ideas now he was in power, war was likely to occur.

First, Hitler wanted to tighten his control over Germany. He demanded yet another general election in March 1933.

Determined to win an overall majority in the Reichstag, he used the police and his own private police and military forces, the SS and the SA, to violently disrupt other parties' campaigns.

Just before election day, the Reichstag building burned down. Hitler blamed the communists. He banned the Communist Party and called on the German people to vote Nazi to save the nation. Even then, he did not win control over the Reichstag.

TOTALITARIANISM

Undaunted, Hitler used troops to overawe the Reichstag, and on 23 March forced it to pass an Enabling Law. This handed Hitler the power to ignore the Weimar Constitution, issue laws without the Reichstag and make agreements with other countries. The Weimar Republic was dead.

Hitler set up a totalitarian state with himself at its head. All political parties except the Nazis were outlawed and trade unions were abolished. Churches were terrorized into accepting the Nazis; education and the media were tightly controlled by the Nazi Party.

All opposition was ruth-lessly dealt with using the SS and the SA. The army approved of most of these actions; Hitler wanted to keep the officers on his side. Before long he was going to need them.

Adolf Hitler (1889–1945)

A number of factors help to explain Hitler's success. He understood the power of terror – his opponents were too frightened to resist. He knew the force of propaganda (talking of the 'stab in the back' in 1918, for example) and appointed the very able Joseph Goebbels to head his propaganda machine. Hitler was determined to get his way by force or through cunning.

That said, many of Hitler's ideas – especially those on race – were fanatical. In normal times he would have been ignored or locked up (as indeed he had been). But the times were not normal. Germany was a desperate country. Was this desperation the real secret of Hitler's success?

LEFT

Adolf Hitler, whose simple ideas for solving his country's problems gained widespread popular appeal.

ABOVE *Ignoring international protests, Japanese forces occupy the Chinese province of Manchuria, 1931–2.*

MANCHURIA

While the Nazis were taking over in Germany, aggression was on the increase elsewhere. In 1931–2 the Japanese overran the northern Chinese province of Manchuria. This was the first major test of the power of the League of Nations, and it failed dismally.

The League's previous failures to halt aggression (for example, when Mussolini seized Corfu in 1923) had been dismissed as 'teething troubles'. There could be no such excuse by 1931. The League condemned Japan and ordered its troops to withdraw. Japan refused. The League set up a commission that suggested that the League itself govern Manchuria. Again, Japan refused and in March 1933 it left the League.

Neither economic nor military sanctions against Japan were feasible. No country could afford such action because of the Depression. Consequently, Japan got away with conquering a rich province of 30 million inhabitants. The League's tattered reputation received a further blow when its Disarmament Conference was abandoned in 1934.

Manchuria: could the Japanese have been stopped?

The Japanese army in Guandong (near Manchuria) was largely independent. Consequently, the invasion of Manchuria surprised the Japanese government almost as much as the rest of the world.

Although the 'Manchurian Incident' was condemned internationally, Tokyo refused to halt the invasion. The League could not act because it said it could not afford troops to enforce its decisions. If the League had spent money on armaments and troops, this spending could have boosted the depressed economies of its member countries. And if League members had gone to war with Japan over Manchuria, might they have halted aggression? Would other countries such as Italy and Germany have dared to seize new countries if they had thought they might be stopped?

ABYSSINIA

Proof that the peaceful spirit of the 1920s was gone for good came in 1935. Like all of Europe outside the Soviet Union, Italy had been hard hit by the Depression. Mussolini needed a grand gesture; he decided to grab a colony to boost Italy's wealth and international standing. His target was the poor and undeveloped African kingdom of Abyssinia (now Ethiopia).

Following a minor border incident, Mussolini's forces invaded Abyssinia in October 1935. Six months later they were in Addis Ababa, the capital. Once more the League of Nations condemned the aggressor – it even arranged some economic sanctions against Italy. Neither action had any effect whatsoever.

By 1936 the idea that the First World War had been the 'war to end all wars' was looking rather hollow. A new world conflict looked increasingly likely.

LEFT *Poorly equipped Abyssinian troops fire at Italian aircraft, 1935. They had no hope against Italian armoured vehicles, aircraft and poison gas.*

ABOVE *Loading bombs aboard Junkers JU87 dive bombers. Coming into service in 1937, the JU87 (better known as the 'Stuka') was at the forefront of Hitler's new air force.*

REARMAMENT

In 1934, a year after leaving the League of Nations, Japan rejected the Washington Naval Treaty, which had limited the size of its navy. This, as well as the conquest of Manchuria, showed Japan's unwillingness to be ordered about by other nations.

Precisely the same thing was happening in Germany. The Treaty of Versailles had limited the German army, and allowed it no air force, large battleships or submarines. For parts of Germany with proud military traditions, such as Prussia, these terms were an embarrassment.

Even during the Weimar Republic era, the Versailles restrictions were broken. The navy conducted secret research into submarines. New surface ships, such as the 'pocket battleships' of the early 1930s, were often larger than their declared size. The secret reconstruction of the German air force, the *Luftwaffe*, was even more impressive. Pilots were trained as civil pilots or as 'sportsmen' glider pilots. The Junkers aircraft company built metal transport planes that could easily be converted to bombers.

INTO THE RHINELAND

Thus, when Hitler came to power in 1933 and set about restoring Germany's military power, he found the foundations were already laid. The work of rearmament continued in secret throughout 1934. After that it was conducted openly, in defiance of the Treaty of Versailles. Britain and France, who had main responsibility for the Treaty, did not intervene. Instead, they too began to rearm. Britain's military expenditure increased six-fold from 1934 to 1939, the same increase as Germany's. France's increased ten-fold.

In 1936 Hitler sent troops into the Rhineland on the border with France. The Versailles and Locarno Treaties had declared the area demilitarized. Britain and France protested but they did not take any further action.

? WHAT IF...

Britain and France had intervened in 1936?

When German troops entered the Rhineland in 1936, Germany was in no position to fight a war. It had virtually no armoured vehicles, no heavy artillery and few aircraft. The Nazis had introduced conscription but the new recruits were poorly trained and ill-equipped. Hitler reckoned he could not fight a major war until 1944.

The reoccupation of the Rhineland by German troops was a gamble – a way of testing Anglo-French resolve. The German soldiers had orders to retreat if they met with any resistance. Since no resistance was offered, Hitler tried further acts of aggression (see page 37). Therefore, had Britain and France actively resisted the Germans in 1936, they might possibly have avoided all-out war.

LEFT *And no one stopped them... Breaking the Treaty of Versailles, German troops march into the Rhineland in 1936. They probably would have withdrawn if challenged.*

APPEASEMENT

After occupying the Rhineland, Hitler continued to rearm. In 1938 he again broke the Treaty of Versailles when he annexed Austria. He went on to claim the Sudetenland, the German-speaking part of western Czechoslovakia, for Germany (see page 39).

Britain and France did nothing to halt this aggression. Indeed, sometimes they seemed to accept it. In 1935, for example, when Hitler denounced the military clauses of the Treaty of Versailles, Britain signed a treaty that allowed Germany to build up its navy. Also in 1935, the British and French foreign ministers secretly agreed to accept Mussolini's conquest of Abyssinia.

This policy of backing down before the fascist dictators is known as 'appeasement'. It is associated with two British prime ministers, Stanley Baldwin (in power 1935–37) and Neville

BELOW *A right-wing youth demonstration in France, February 1936. There was a struggle between right and left-wing parties in France and Britain as well as in Germany in the 1930s.*

? PEOPLE IN QUESTION

Neville Chamberlain (1869–1940)

Chamberlain (1937–40). At the time Winston Churchill and others condemned it as cowardly. By giving in, Churchill argued, Britain was only putting off an inevitable war.

FOR AND AGAINST APPEASEMENT

Hitler and Mussolini took hope from the apparent Anglo-French weakness, and continued their aggression. When Britain and France finally declared war on Germany in September 1939, Hitler was surprised. Having had his own way since 1933, he did not believe anyone would ever stand up to him.

Few British prime ministers have been more bitterly criticized than Chamberlain. In 1938 he accepted Hitler's *Anschluss* (union) with Austria but threatened war when the German leader menaced the Sudetenland, the German-speaking part of Czechoslovakia. After crisis talks in Munich, Germany, Hitler agreed to make no more land claims. Chamberlain returned home a national hero. He had, he said, brought 'peace in our time'. Yet Hitler broke the agreement only months later.

In Chamberlain's defence, what else could he have done? Britain and France did not have the power at that time to save Czechoslovakia by force. Moreover, in 1938 few British or French people were prepared to risk another major war to defend a distant and little-known nation.

On the other hand, appeasement can be defended. Firstly, many people hated the thought of another war. In 1933, in a famous debate, Oxford University students voted not to fight for their country. Secondly, the longer a war was delayed, the more time there was to rearm. Thirdly, by the 1930s it was widely recognized that the Treaty of Versailles had been unjust. Perhaps appeasement was a sensible attempt to put right the wrongs of the past?

CHAPTER 4

The Rising Sun

U ntil the second half of the 19th century Japan had been largely isolated from the rest of the world. From 1868 onwards it entered a period of rapid Westernization. This involved remodelling most aspects of Japanese life – including government, education and industry – along Western lines.

? PEOPLE IN QUESTION

Hirohito (1901–1989): warmonger?

For much of Japan's history the emperor was an all-powerful figure. However, after the Westernization process of the 19th century, the emperor became more of a figurehead. He simply signed his agreement to his ministers' policies.

Nevertheless, many Japanese still regarded their emperor as a god, and their real leader. They would do whatever he ordered. Indeed, on one or two key occasions, such as when he opposed an attempted army coup in 1936, Hirohito did influence Japanese politics. Why, therefore, did he not publicly oppose his country's warmongers in the 1930s? Was it because he secretly approved of their plans? Or, more likely, because he was powerless to stop them and did not want to damage his reputation in the attempt?

ABOVE RIGHT *The Crown Prince Hirohito of Japan (left) and Britain's Prince of Wales (second from left) at a dinner in London in 1921. Britain and Japan, deadly enemies in World War II, had been allied since 1902.*

A TROUBLED WORLD POWER

Japan made remarkable progress. By the early 20th century it was a world power, and by the 1920s the country's ambition was beginning to worry the United States (see page 52).

Nevertheless, Japan was beset by fundamental problems. First, the military wanted more control over East Asia. Second, the elected government found it hard to control the military and the big businesses that profited from military spending. Third, nationalists demanded that Japan give up corrupt Western ways and return to traditional Japanese customs, including giving the emperor absolute power.

JAPANESE NATIONALISM

These trends grew more pronounced when Japan was hit by the Depression. The value of Japanese exports fell by almost 50 per cent to 1,426 million yen. One of the biggest price cuts (about 75 per cent) was in raw silk, a key Japanese export. As in Germany, unemployment and unrest spread, and extreme groups and ideas grew in popularity. A spate of political assassinations made matters worse.

This was the situation in which a nationalist Japanese army led by Ishiwara Kanji moved from its base in Kwantung, seized Mukden and then swiftly occupied the whole of Manchuria (see page 24). The action had been taken without the permission of the government. Nevertheless, to save face it backed the occupation and so gave official approval to the new aggression.

ABOVE *Japanese tea pickers, 1920. Despite its technological progress, Japan remained a very traditional society. This meant obedience to the emperor and the government.*

JAPAN AND CHINA

As we saw on page 4, the conflicts that developed into the Second World War began with a war between Japan and China in 1937. Why, since Japan had invaded the Chinese province of Manchuria six years earlier, had the war not started then?

There were two reasons why China did not react more strongly to the attack on Manchuria. First, it hoped the League of Nations would sort the matter out (see page 24). Second, the country was torn by a bitter civil war and in no state to unite against an invader.

CHINA'S PROBLEMS

The roots of China's weakness went far back. From the mid-19th century onwards, Western powers bullied China and forced it to hand over key ports. (Hong Kong, for instance, became a British colony in 1842.) China's ancient system of government, based around an all-powerful emperor, was unable to cope and in 1911 it was overthrown in revolution.

BELOW *China in turmoil – troops defy orders and join the revolution that overturned imperial rule in 1911.*

Chiang Kai-shek (1887–1975)

Chiang Kai-Shek had been trained as a soldier in both Japan and the Soviet Union. These two influences seemed to reflect the different sides of his character: his wish for personal power and his desire to do what was best for his country.

Chiang Kai-Shek's time in Japan fed his desire for personal glory. The Soviet experience appealed to his wish to modernize China, to give it an up-to-date industrial and transport system like the USSR. Sadly, although he started his career with high ideals, power seemed to corrupt his idealism. The communist threat to his personal position blinded him to the more real danger from Japan. He became an intolerant and harsh leader of a corrupt regime.

ABOVE *The Chinese leader Chiang Kai-Shek, whose dreams of creating a fairer society were swallowed up by personal ambition.*

After years of feuding between various 'warlords', in 1928 Chiang Kai-shek, who was head of the National People's Party (KMT), established a National Government in Nanking. Chiang Kai-Shek wished to modernize China and had little sympathy with the country's huge peasant majority.

CHIANG KAI-SHEK AND THE COMMUNISTS

The Chinese Communist Party (founded 1921) was inspired by the Soviet experience. But its leaders, especially Mao Zedong, decided that success in China could be achieved only with the backing of the peasants. Chiang Kai-shek did not want the CCP to take over his movement, and in 1927 tried to crush it.

A series of brutal campaigns failed to break the communist resistance. Moreover, Chiang Kai-shek was so obsessed with the communist threat that he allowed the Japanese aggression in Manchuria to pass without serious challenge. This pleased the Japanese government.

33

ABOVE *A machine-gun post on the Great Wall of China during the Sino-Japanese War (1937–45).*

THE JAPANESE WAY

The Japanese government's failure to condemn the invasion of Manchuria had lasting consequences. Democracy was discredited. The right-wing military, on the other hand, was praised for restoring national pride. (Incidentally, Japan did not formally take over Manchuria as a colony, but set up a 'puppet' state – Manchuko – headed by the last Chinese emperor, Pu Yi.)

The Manchurian success boosted the popularity of the 'Japanese Way' – great respect for the emperor, fierce nationalism and a belief that Japan had a historic mission to lead Asia. Censorship increased; so did spending on armaments. In 1936 Japan entered into the Anti-Comintern (anti-communist) Pact with Hitler. As spending rose and Japan's economy improved, nationalism was associated with a return of prosperity.

WAR IN ASIA

Taking advantage of China's civil war (see page 33), Japan extended its influence south and west of Manchuria. It occupied the province of Jehol in 1933 and in 1935 tried to establish a puppet state of North China, including Beijing. During 1937 the CCP and the KMT finally united against their common enemy, Japan.

On 7 July 1937, a minor clash occurred between Japanese troops exercising near Beijing and a Chinese garrison. Chiang Kai-shek responded by ordering reinforcements to attack the intruders. This resulted in the outbreak of a war that lasted until Japan surrendered to the USA and its allies in 1945.

Japan's efficient Guandong Army swept all before it, seizing the important cities of Tianjin, Beijing, Nanking (Chiang Kai-Shek's capital) and Shanghai. It justified its conquests as 'liberating' China from the influence of the USSR (through the CCP) and the USA (through the KMT, which had strong US backing).

? EVENT IN QUESTION

When did World War II really start: 1937 or 1939?

Was the outbreak of the Sino-Japanese War in 1937 the real beginning of World War II? The traditional date for the outbreak of the Second World War is September 1939, when Hitler attacked Poland and Britain and France declared war on Germany. As this involved Britain and France's worldwide empires, one could say the war of 1939 was a world war. However, the fighting was largely limited to Europe.

If 1939 is a valid date, so also is 1937. The date signals the beginning of Japan's programme of military expansion. This came to involve virtually all Asia, as well as the USA and European imperial powers. On the other hand, the fighting in China was not part of a formal war. Neither China nor Japan declared war on each other until after the Japanese raid on Pearl Harbor in December 1941.

BELOW *Japanese marines celebrate the capture of Shanghai in 1937.*

CHAPTER 5

Towards the Brink

Events in Europe by 1936 were taking a similarly violent turn to those in the Far East. Hitler had reoccupied the Rhineland and Mussolini was completing his conquest of Abyssinia. General Franco had plunged Spain into a bloody civil war.

ANSCHLUSS

By the end of the year the outlook was gloomier still. Hitler and Mussolini had formed a coalition, the Rome–Berlin Axis. Japan and Germany had signed the Anti-Comintern Pact against the USSR. In response, Europe's democracies were rearming fast. In 1935 Britain spent £17 million on its air force; by 1939 this had risen to £133 million.

BELOW *One people, one leader: the Reichstag glories in the unification of Germany and Austria, March 1938.*

The Rome–Berlin Axis was important for Hitler's plans regarding Austria, his native land. He had long talked of *Anschluss*, a union between Germany and Austria. The two states shared a language and similar culture. Until 1866 they had been part of the same German Confederation. In 1918 a majority of Austrians had voted in favour of *Anschluss* but the Treaty of Versailles had banned the union between them.

TALK OF WAR

Hitler had tried to bring about *Anschluss* in 1934. Austrian Nazis, with German encouragement, had murdered the Austrian chancellor, Engelbert Dollfuss. When a full Nazi take-over seemed possible, Mussolini moved troops to the Austro-Italian border and warned Hitler off. Hitler had to abandon his plans.

Spanish Civil War, 1936–9: a dress rehearsal?

ABOVE *Fighters from Spain's Republican army, 1936, who fought General Franco's fascist forces.*

Once the Rome–Berlin Axis was formed, Mussolini would no longer oppose Hitler. Nazi forces moved into Austria in March 1938. The Austrian government, unable to control Nazi demonstrations, had announced a vote on the *Anschluss* question. German soldiers swept in before the vote could be held. The majority of Austrians seemed to welcome the move, although liberals and Austrian Jews feared the worst.

This time round, Mussolini made no attempt to prevent *Anschluss*. Britain and France protested and boosted their rearmament programmes. The talk in Europe was increasingly of war.

In July 1936 the right-wing General Francisco Franco launched a military coup against Spain's left-wing Popular Front government, beginning a civil war.

Hitler and Mussolini openly supported Franco with men and military equipment. The Soviet Union backed the anti-Franco Republicans. The Republicans were also supported by thousands of volunteers from Britain, France and other democratic countries. Franco eventually won the war.

Was this conflict a dress rehearsal for the larger European war of 1939–45? The style of warfare – bombing and the widespread use of armoured vehicles – was a sign of things to come. It was a war between fascism and democracy. Nevertheless, this was very much a Spanish war, between the forces of traditional Spain and the democratic forces of progress.

CZECHOSLOVAKIA

The success of the *Anschluss* was deeply worrying for much of Europe. It showed that Hitler was intent on expanding his Nazi regime, the Third Reich. Britain and France, the key powers behind the Treaty of Versailles, had again failed to uphold it.

The next crisis, over Czechoslovakia later in 1938, brought Europe close to war. Czechoslovakia had been created in 1918 out of parts of the old Austrian Empire. Contrary to the suggestion of its name, only 66 per cent of its population were Czechs and Slovaks. There were also Germans (22 per cent), Hungarians (5 per cent) and Poles (0.7 per cent).

RIGHT *Break free with the Nazis: a poster urging the Germans of the Czech Sudetenland to vote yes ('Ja') to the Nazi Party.*

THE SUDETENLAND

Most of Czechoslovakia's 3 million Germans lived near the frontier with Germany, in the Sudetenland region of north-west Bohemia. In 1938 Hitler made it clear that he wanted to bring the Sudeten Germans into his Reich.

As a minority within Czechoslovakia, the Sudeten Germans were treated unfairly. They were denied good jobs, for example. In the general election of 1935 the fascist Sudeten German Party, led by Konrad Henlein, won the support of almost 65 per cent of Sudeten Germans. This put the British and French governments in a difficult position. Versailles had supported self-determination – each nationality deciding its own future. If the Sudeten Germans wished to unite with Germany, who had the right to stop them?

Over the summer of 1938 Henlein stirred up Nazi-style protests in the Sudetenland. Hitler responded with war-like statements in favour of his fellow Germans. The Czech president, Edvard Benes, was determined not to be bullied and looked to Britain and France for political and even military support. The latter, of course, would mean war.

RIGHT *Germans in Moravia, Czechoslovakia welcome the Nazi take-over in March 1939.*

? EVENT IN QUESTION

The creation of Czechoslovakia, 1919: a recipe for disaster?

Two new countries were created in 1919, Czechoslovakia and Yugoslavia. Both now no longer exist. This calls into question the wisdom of the nation-making process.

A nation is a complex mix of culture, language, geography and history. Together they produce a sense of common identity. Czechoslovakia's different nationalities were always going to make it hard for the nation to hold together. The situation was made more difficult because it was pieced together from separate provinces of the Austrian Empire: Moravia, Bohemia and part of Silesia, each with separate traditions.

In accepting the state of Czechoslovakia in 1919, had the Versailles peacemakers created a new problem? Or perhaps there wouldn't have been difficulties if it weren't for other factors, such as the Nazis stirring up nationalism among the Sudeten Germans?

NAZI PRESSURE

Hitler prepared for an armed invasion of the Sudetenland in autumn 1938. In early September, under pressure from Britain and France, President Benes of Czechoslovakia granted all the demands of the Sudeten Germans. Hitler said this was not enough: he wanted to occupy the Sudetenland at once. Meanwhile, the Polish and Hungarian governments were asking to take over those parts of Czechoslovakia inhabited by their people.

By the middle of September the situation was perilous. The French, who had guaranteed Czechoslovakia's frontiers at Locarno (see page 14), agreed to stick to their guarantee. They also said Britain and the Soviet Union (which also had a treaty with Czechoslovakia) would stand by the Czechs. Once again Europe prepared for war.

MUNICH AGREEMENT

No war came. Germany was not ready, nor was Britain, France or the Soviet Union. No one (except President Benes) thought Czechoslovakia worth fighting over. On 29 September Chamberlain flew to Germany for the third time for face-to-face talks with Hitler, which took place in Munich. The French premier, Edouard Daladier, was there. So too was Benito Mussolini. Although now committed to Hitler, he posed as a neutral go-between. Significantly, there was no Czech or Soviet presence at the talks.

It was decided that the areas of Czechoslovakia inhabited by Germans, Hungarians and Poles were to be surrendered immediately to Germany, Hungary and Poland respectively. The Czechs, who had not been consulted, were told they would receive no support if they resisted. In return, the powers guaranteed the frontiers of the reduced Czechoslovakia.

Hitler claimed the Sudetenland was his last territorial claim in Europe. Taking him at his word, Neville Chamberlain flew home to London a hero and made his famous declaration that he had brought 'peace in our time'.

? WHAT IF...

Britain and France had backed President Benes?

In the autumn of 1938, Hitler talked of 'smashing' Czechoslovakia. Did he mean it, or was it merely boastful talk intended to scare his opponents into granting what he wanted? This was the view of the well-known historian A.J.P. Taylor.

An alternative view, put forward by Alan Bullock and other historians, is that Hitler kept his options open. He wanted the Sudetenland without war if possible, but he was prepared for a fight if necessary. Interestingly, his generals advised against going to war.

So if Britain and France had stood by President Benes and rejected Hitler's demands, he might well have attacked the Sudetenland. The Allies would have declared war on Hitler, beginning a major European war in 1938, perhaps with the USSR on the Allies' side from the start.

LEFT *The Munich conference. From left to right: Neville Chamberlain, Edouard Daladier, Hitler, Mussolini and Mussolini's foreign minister, Count Ciano.*

41

SLIDING TOWARDS WAR

The Munich Agreement left Czechoslovakia a poor, divided country, having lost some 70 per cent of its heavy industry. If the Germans, Poles and Hungarians had been allowed to leave Czechoslovakia, the Slovaks now asked, why not them? The country was breaking up.

Hitler seized the moment. He offered to help Czechoslovakia's new president, Emil Hácha, by sending in German troops to maintain law and order. Hácha reluctantly agreed and in March 1939 Nazi forces occupied the entire country. Britain and France protested but did nothing. Since the Czech frontiers had not been violated – the Germans had been invited in – the Munich Agreement had not been broken. Days later, Hitler forced the Lithuanians to allow him to take over the port of Memel.

BELOW *Hitler driving in an open car through Brno during the Nazi take-over of Czechoslovakia in March 1939.*

It was now clear that Hitler was laying the foundations of his huge new Reich. Next he looked east, to the Baltic city of Danzig. In 1919 this largely German-populated city had been made a free state, under League of Nations protection, to give Poland access to a port. Twenty years later Danzig's population was eager to join Hitler's Germany. But the Poles refused to negotiate a handover. Hitler planned to attack Poland.

ABOVE *Gearing up for war: British armament workers making shells in the 1930s. Britain had begun to re-arm as early as 1936.*

THE PACT OF STEEL

British and French behaviour at Munich persuaded Hitler that neither would fight him. This was a serious miscalculation. The mood in both countries had changed. By the summer of 1939, 87 per cent of Britons and 76 per cent of French people favoured war if Hitler attacked Poland. Rearmament was proceeding fast, too – the Anglo-French output of tanks and aircraft now exceeded Germany's.

Before he attacked, Hitler needed to make allies. First he secured Italy with a full alliance called the Pact of Steel.

? EVENT IN QUESTION

The Pact of Steel, 22 May 1939: a significant step on the path to war?

When Hitler first came to power his relations with Mussolini were strained. This was most apparent when Mussolini blocked Hitler's first attempt at *Anschluss* in 1934 (see page 36). By 1939, however, the two fascist powers were united in a bond that only war would break.

The border between Austria and Italy had been a scene of fierce fighting in World War I. Hitler wanted to remove any possibility of an attack by Italy before engaging in a war in northern Europe. From this point of view, the Pact of Steel was a step towards European war. However, Hitler had little regard for Mussolini's military might. Perhaps he would have attacked Poland even without a pact with Italy?

ABOVE *Grim-faced prisoners in one of Stalin's labour camps, 1932. By 1939 so many able citizens had been killed or were in prison that the USSR was in no fit state for war.*

THE SOVIET UNION

Tragically, during the first eight months of 1939 almost all Europeans knew there was a war coming, yet no one seemed able to prevent it.

Neither Britain nor France wanted war, although they were prepared to fight if they had to. Poland certainly didn't want war. Even Hitler wanted only a short, sharp fight with Poland to demonstrate the strength of the new Germany. He did not want a major European conflict. In the end, the key to what happened lay not with any of these countries, but with the Soviet Union.

Starting in April 1939, Britain, with French backing, held talks with the Soviet Union. The British wanted a one-way alliance: a promise of Soviet support against Germany if necessary. The Soviets sought a two-way alliance: each side to come to the other's aid if called on. Britain refused to commit itself to supporting the Soviet Union against Germany, partly because of distrust of the communist government. In August the talks fizzled out.

NAZI-SOVIET NON-AGGRESSION PACT

An important opportunity had slipped by. If Hitler had faced a united front of the Soviet Union, Britain and France, he might have pulled back from his Polish adventure. A war on more than one front was to be avoided at all costs. Hitler now came to an agreement with the USSR himself.

The Nazi-Soviet Non-Aggression Pact of 23 August 1939 was a diplomatic revolution. Fascism and communism were opposing political ideas. Now, suddenly, an agreement was forged: the Soviets undertook to remain neutral while Hitler had his way in eastern Europe. In return, Hitler allowed them free rein in the Baltic states.

? EVENT IN QUESTION

Nazi-Soviet Pact, 23 August 1939: cynical or practical?

The Nazi-Soviet Pact made sense to both sides. Hitler was free to attack Poland in the knowledge that the Soviet Union would remain neutral. That, he estimated, would ensure that Britain and France would not dare intervene. The Pact bought time for the USSR, which was unprepared for war. Stalin had recently removed 80 per cent of the Red Army's colonels and 90 per cent of its generals because he suspected them of opposing him. Secondly, the Pact allowed Soviet forces to enter Estonia, Latvia, Lithuania, part of Poland and Finland. This gave the USSR a buffer of small states along its western frontier.

Nevertheless, from Hitler's point of view the Pact was deeply cynical. He had not abandoned his idea of expanding eastwards beyond Poland to give 'living space' to the German people, merely postponed it.

ABOVE *Von Ribbentrop (Germany) and Molotov (USSR) at a meeting in September 1939.*

CHAPTER 6

War in Europe

Throughout August 1939 Hitler tried to get Britain and France to repeat their Munich climbdown and force Poland to accept his demands. In the end he ordered his forces to attack Poland on 1 September. Britain and France gave Hitler an ultimatum to withdraw from Poland. He refused. To Hitler's surprise, they then declared war on Germany on 3 September.

ABOVE *Britons read of the German attack on Poland on 1 September 1939. Britain and France declared war on Germany two days later.*

THE PHONEY WAR

There were now two major areas of conflict in the world, Asia and Europe. In Asia Japan was fighting China; in Europe Germany was overwhelming Poland and the Soviet Union was moving into its new sphere of influence in eastern Europe (see page 45).

At the end of 1939, Finland was fighting a bitter war against the Soviet Union to resist occupation. But the other European campaigns had petered out. Britain and France had exchanged occasional air raids with Germany and there had been some conflict at sea. However, as Britain and France had decided they could not intervene to save Poland (which received not one rifle of British aid), the phoney war saw no significant military action in the west.

At this stage there was no world war. The British Empire, although wary of Japan's links with Hitler and Mussolini (see page 36), was not engaged on a global scale. The Soviet Union was involved only in Finland. The United States, the most powerful nation on earth, was at war with no one. The next question, therefore, is how these various conflicts expanded into a Second World War.

Joseph Stalin (1879–1953)

For many years, hard facts about the rule of Iosef Dzhugashvili, otherwise known as Stalin ('Man of Steel'), were difficult to come by. In 1948, three years after Stalin had fought with the Allies in World War II, the historian Isaac Deutscher wrote:

'Stalin cannot be classed with Hitler, among the tyrants whose record is one of worthlessness and futility... Stalin has been both the leader and the exploiter of a tragic, self-contradictory, but creative revolution.'

(Stalin, Pelican, 1966, p.612)

After Stalin's death and especially since the collapse of the USSR in 1990–91, more information about Stalin's rule became available. It has been calculated that his policies were responsible for maybe as many as 40 million deaths. As a result, as historians Jon Nichol and Keith Shephard suggest, he is frequently compared with Hitler as 'the greatest mass murderer in the world's history'.

(Russia, Blackwell, 1986, p.42)

LEFT Joseph Stalin, photographed in the 1920s. Some would say he was just as bad as Hitler – or worse.

ABOVE *German troops
enter Paris, June 1940.
France came to terms
with the Nazis and set
up 'Vichy France'
under its own
semi-independent
government.*

THE WAR SPREADS

In 1940 the wars in Europe and Asia expanded considerably, but not yet into a world war. Hitler's long-term aim was to carve out 'living-space' in north-eastern Europe for the German 'master race'. Before he could do this, he needed to secure his western frontier. In April Scandinavia was drawn into the conflict when Hitler attacked Denmark and Norway (Sweden remained neutral). Of greater significance was the sudden and successful German attack on the Netherlands, Belgium, Luxembourg and France, which began in May.

The total defeat of France and the real possibility of an invasion of Britain had widespread consequences. First, picking up the scent of victory, Mussolini joined the war in June. This spread the war to North Africa, where the Italians attacked British forces, and to Greece, which Mussolini invaded in October.

Winston Churchill (1874–1965)

Britain's wartime leader, Churchill, had long been warning against the danger of Hitler's aims in Europe. He had called the Munich Agreement 'a total and unmitigated [thorough] defeat'. History proved his warnings justified. But could his fellow politicians have been blamed for not listening to him?

By 1938 Churchill had enjoyed a spectacular career – journalist, writer, army officer, prisoner of war, First Lord of the Admiralty, Home Secretary and Chancellor of the Exchequer. Nevertheless, he had several times proved hot-headed in judgement, for example when he spoke in favour of the risky Gallipoli Campaign in World War I. By 1936 most people saw him as a spent force; he had not held a government position since 1929. It is not surprising that many people dismissed his anti-Nazi remarks.

ABOVE *Winston Churchill (left) and General Bernard Montgomery, one of his leading commanders.*

THE GREATER EAST ASIA CO-PROSPERITY SPHERE

Fascist successes in Europe prompted Japan to take advantage of the weakness of the colonial powers in Asia. Having set up a puppet government in the part of China it occupied, Japan announced plans for the Greater East Asia Co-Prosperity Sphere. This was a dignified term for a new Japanese empire in Asia. The Japanese now threatened British control in Burma (Myanmar) and occupied the northern part of the French colony of Indo-China (Vietnam).

As we saw, in 1936 Japan had signed an anti-communist pact with Hitler and Mussolini. Not surprisingly, the Nazi-Soviet Non-Aggression Pact horrified the Japanese. The Anti-Comintern Pact now lapsed. In September 1940, with the war expanding, the Japanese reached a new agreement with Germany and Italy, the Tripartite Pact. This brought the three nations together as military allies for the first time. The move was vital in the development of a worldwide war.

ABOVE *A British soldier amid the ruins of battle in North Africa, 1941. The Italians had attacked British forces in the region.*

1941

1941 was a pivotal year. First, the Soviet Union entered the fray; second, the USA became heavily involved in both the Asian and European wars. By the end of December 1941, therefore, the fighting going on in different parts of the world had merged into the global conflict we call the Second World War.

The European conflict spread into Yugoslavia, across North Africa and into French-controlled Syria and Lebanon, and Iraq. Hungary went to war alongside Germany when the latter attacked Yugoslavia in April 1941. Romania also sided with Germany and found itself drawn into the fighting in Russia in the summer of that year.

BARBAROSSA

The war came to Romania when it participated in Operation Barbarossa – the German invasion of the Soviet Union. Launched on 22 June, it was the largest military campaign ever conducted. Moreover, it entangled Hitler in a war he could not win.

Hitler's motives for the war were partly emotional. In his eyes the Slavic people (which included Russians) were among the lowest racial groups. As the German master race needed 'living space', the obvious place to find it was among the open spaces of European Russia and the Ukraine.

Operation Barbarossa

Hitler invaded the USSR with an army of 3.05 million men. The campaign, which lasted until 1945, was the most destructive the world has ever seen, and it proved Hitler's undoing. Why, therefore, did he begin it?

Hitler himself said it was to get at Britain:
'With Russia smashed, Britain's last hope would be shattered.'

Most historians, however, agree with David Williamson:
'On balance it seems more likely that Hitler's long term... ideological hatred of Bolshevism [communism] and his determination to gain lebensraum *[living space]... played the key role in his decision to attack Russia.'*

(Both in *War and Peace: International Relations 1914–45*, Hodder and Stoughton, 1994, p.132)

More rationally, Hitler believed that war between the two conflicting ideologies – fascism and communism – was inevitable, so it was better to strike first. Moreover, the USSR was rich in resources the Nazis needed, especially oil. Finally, Hitler seriously miscalculated how difficult it would be to overcome the Soviets. He believed he would be master of Soviet Russia by the end of the year. Overconfident, he neglected to arrange for Japan to attack Russia from the east at the same time.

ABOVE *Operation Barbarossa: German tanks sweep across the western Soviet Union in the summer of 1941.*

CHAPTER 7

World War

It was Japan that had set in motion the train of aggression that led to World War II. Japan first defied the League of Nations by conquering Manchuria, and Japan began the first of the wars (with China) that eventually merged into world war. It was perhaps appropriate, therefore, that Japan struck the blow that brought the USA into the war and so produced global warfare.

US–JAPANESE RELATIONS

The US government had been uneasy about Japan's foreign policy intentions for a long time. It had also been concerned about developments in China, where the USA backed the KMT against Mao's communists (see page 35). When China and Japan went to war in 1937, the USA increased aid to Chiang Kai-Shek, now China's official war leader. Clearly, this angered the Japanese.

Japan's Tripartite Pact with Hitler and Mussolini in 1940 further damaged US–Japanese relations. At the time the US government was doing all it could, short of going to war, to help those fighting fascism. The announcement of the Greater East Asia Co-Prosperity Sphere heightened US suspicions that Japan's real interest was empire building. A large undemocratic Japanese empire in East Asia would be a direct threat to US commercial interests and security in the Pacific.

INDO-CHINA

In July 1941 Japanese troops moved further into the French colony of Indo-China. President Roosevelt stepped up US pressure on Japan. Japanese assets (money, property and businesses) in the USA were 'frozen', meaning they could not be used.

? PEOPLE IN QUESTION

President F.D. Roosevelt (1882–1945)

In 1940 Roosevelt was re-elected President of the USA on a promise to keep out of the war. He almost certainly realized this would be an impossible promise to keep. In addition, he wanted the USA to play a part in the war to fight fascism.

Roosevelt put Japan under pressure with the oil embargo, insisting that it would be lifted only if Japan agreed to leave Indo-China and China. The Japanese government could not survive for long with the oil embargo. It could either withdraw from the countries it had invaded, which would mean losing face, or fight back. Japan attacked the USA and the US declared war.

So did the politician who was elected as a man of peace betray the voters?

Even harder for Japan, the US government placed an embargo (a ban) on the sale of vital US oil to Japan. At the same time, diplomats met to try to sort out peacefully the differences between the two Pacific powers.

BELOW *Japanese citizens in the USA were held in camps and had to swear allegiance to the US flag.*

ABOVE *Hideki Tojo*
(1884–1948), the
Japanese prime minister
who gave the order for
the attack on Pearl
Harbor. He was found
guilty of war crimes and
hanged in 1948.

PRIME MINISTER TOJO

On 16 October 1941 Hideki Tojo became prime minister of Japan. Tojo was a militarist: a devoted servant of the emperor. He believed in the supremacy of the Japanese people and was a keen supporter of the alliance with the European fascists. As prime minister he discussed with the generals and admirals what Japan should do if it found itself at war with the United States. The war, he felt, was bound to come sooner rather than later.

FIRST STRIKE

Japan's leaders decided that to wait for war before putting their plans into operation would be foolish. The USA had a more powerful navy than Japan, and was much wealthier. The only hope for the smaller country was to strike first and to strike hard. The target chosen by Commander-in-Chief Yamamoto was the US naval base of Pearl Harbor in Hawaii.

On 7 December, with no warning whatsoever, 353 Japanese planes appeared in the skies over Pearl Harbor. The attack lasted two hours, destroying hundreds of aircraft and sinking 18 ships, including 5 battleships. US casualties numbered 2,403; 64 Japanese died. Fortunately for the USA, the aircraft carriers were not in port that day. The USA and Britain declared war on Japan the next day.

WORLD WAR

Although it placed a huge new strain on their resources, on 11 December Germany and Italy declared war on the USA. This completed the circle. The Axis powers – Germany, Japan, Italy and their allies – were ranged against the Allies – Britain, the Soviet Union, the USA and their allies. It was a global conflict of far greater scope than that of 1914–18. Indeed, it was a war the like of which the world had never seen before.

The Japanese Attack on Pearl Harbor: was it inevitable?

Some historians believe that the Japanese attack on Pearl Harbor was bound to happen. It was, argued the historian J.G. Utley, the inevitable clash between the Japanese and American views of the world. The two could not co-exist, so conflict was bound to arise. The attack on Pearl Harbor was significant only because it launched that conflict.

A more common view was that the reasons for the attack on Pearl Harbor lay in the chain of events of 1941. Indeed, it may be argued that the USA itself was partly to blame for the attack for forcing Japan into a corner over the oil embargo.

ABOVE *The deed that brought the USA into the war: badly damaged ships of the US Navy after the surprise attack by Japanese planes.*

CHAPTER 8

The Final Analysis

Immediately World War II finished, historians began asking why it had happened. The most obvious answer – very popular in 1945 – was to blame individuals.

BLAME HITLER?

One person stood out: Adolf Hitler. His attacks had started the fighting in Europe, first in Poland, then in France and the Low Countries, then in the Soviet Union. If a villain was needed, he was the obvious choice. Had he died in the 'flu epidemic that swept Europe after World War I, the history of the 20th century might have been radically different.

There are several drawbacks to the simple 'blame Hitler' theory. First, he did not start the war in the Far East. It is less easy to find an individual to blame for what happened there. Tojo, perhaps? Yet he was no dictator, only the head of a cabinet that took decisions together.

BELOW *Returning home: Soviet citizens pick their way through the debris of war after the withdrawal of the German invaders, 1944.*

The outbreak of the Second World War: was Hitler personally responsible?

The British historian A.J.P. Taylor was the first to argue that Hitler was a relatively normal politician who generally acted rationally (*The Origins of the Second World War*, Hamish Hamilton, 1961). The history of the 1930s was too complex, he argued, for a single individual to exert great influence.

In the 1960s Taylor's thesis was challenged by historians such as Hugh Trevor-Roper and Alan Bullock (*Hitler, A Study in Tyranny*, Hamlyn 2nd edition, 1964). Bullock wrote:

'...so far as what actually happened is concerned... the evidence seems to me to leave no doubt that no other man played a role in the Nazi revolution or in the history of the Third Reich remotely comparable to that of Adolf Hitler.' (p.803)

BELOW *Britons emerge into the daylight after a bombing raid, 1940. By 1945 enemy action had destroyed some 2 million British homes.*

COMPLEX CAUSES

Second, blaming Hitler can only partly explain what happened. For example, a near-madman like Hitler could have come to power only after the Germans' humiliation at Versailles and the devastation of the Great Depression. Perhaps, instead of Hitler, we should blame the politicians who drew up the Versailles Treaty or the economists and politicians who allowed the world economy to nosedive in 1929.

Alternatively, did the blame lie with von Papen and Hindenburg, the men who put Hitler in power in 1933? Had they acted differently, might there have been no World War II? Or Chamberlain, Daladier and the other appeasers? Or even American politicians who kept their country out of world affairs until it was too late? Clearly, blaming individuals is easy but it does not fully explain why major events happen.

ABOVE *The frightening rise of Hitler to power: members of the Hitler Youth welcome their leader to a rally, 1938.*

THE STORM OF WAR

The war that reached its full global fury in December 1941 crept up on the world like a tempest. At first there were just clouds on the horizon: German humiliation at Versailles and US isolationism, China's weakness and Japan's growing nationalism. The sky darkened with the rise of extreme right-wing groups in Italy, Japan and Germany, and the Great Depression.

Then came the first drops of rain: the failure of the League of Nations and its key members to stand up to right-wing aggression in Manchuria (1931), Abyssinia (1935), China (1937) and Czechoslovakia (1938). By 1939 there was a storm: war in Europe and China. Finally, in 1941 this developed into full-blown tempest: Hitler's attack on the Soviet Union and Japan's attack on Pearl Harbor.

AN INEVITABLE CONFLICT?

Put like this, it looks as if the Second World War was inevitable. Indeed, as far back as 1919 some sort of second conflict in Europe was predicted (see page 9). Similarly, once the Japanese had gone into Manchuria in 1931, a major confrontation in the Far East

? EVENT IN QUESTION

The Munich Agreement, 1938 – changing views

The policy of appeasement, of which the Munich Agreement was the best example, shows how attitudes change with time.

On 27 September 1938 Chamberlain explained the logic of his policy:
'How horrible, fantastic, incredible it is that we should be digging trenches... here because of a quarrel in a faraway country between people of whom we know nothing.'

After the war Winston Churchill scorned the appeasers, recalling what he said at the time:
'The partition of Czechoslovakia under pressure from England and France amounts to the complete surrender of the Western Democracies to the Nazi threat of force.'

David Williamson sums up more recent thinking:
'Now historians see appeasement as 'a central episode in [Britain's] protracted [long drawn-out] retreat from an untenable [unable to be held] world power status' (Robbins) and as an unavoidable consequence of her economic and military weakness.'

(*War and Peace: International Relations 1914–45*, Hodder and Stoughton, 1994)

BELOW *Flags of participating countries fly outside the building in San Francisco, USA where the United Nations was founded in 1945.*

was on the cards: neither the Soviet Union nor the USA could accept China being in the hands of another power.

KEY MOMENTS

Yet the war was not inevitable. At any point something could have happened – the death of a leading politician, for example – that could have changed the way things developed. On many occasions developments depended on key decisions or events that might well have gone the other way. Looking back, we can see their significance. But the future was as obscure then as it is today.

1914–18
First World War.

1917
Communists come to power in Soviet Union.

1918
NOVEMBER: End of First World War.

1918–22
Russian Civil War.

1919
Weimar Republic founded in Germany.
Treaty of Versailles produces post-war settlement for Western Europe.
Right-wing National Essence Society founded in Japan.

1919
League of Nations founded.

1921
German reparations fixed at 132 billion gold marks.

1922
The fascist leader Mussolini comes to power in Italy.
Washington Naval Treaty limits size of major powers' navies. It recognizes Japan as major power in Far East.

1923
French and Belgian troops occupy the Ruhr district of Germany.

1924
Dawes Plans eases the burden of reparations on Germany.

1925
European frontiers guaranteed at Locarno.

1926
Germany joins the League of Nations.

1928
Stalin in power in the Soviet Union.
Chiang Kai-shek, head of the KMT, comes to power in China.
Kellogg-Briand Pact renounces war as an instrument of policy.

1929
Young Plan further eases the burden of Germany's reparations.
OCTOBER: Wall Street Crash signals beginning of the Great Depression.

1930
The Depression worsens. France begins to build defences – the Maginot Line – along its border with Germany.

1931
Japanese begin conquest of Manchuria.

1932
JULY: Nazis most popular party in German elections.

1932–4
World Disarmament Conference.

1933
Hitler become chancellor of Germany (January) and the Reichstag passes the Enabling Law (March); end of the Weimar Republic.
Japan and Germany leave the League of Nations.

1934
Soviet Union joins League of Nations.
Mussolini foils Hitler's attempt at *Anschluss*.

1935
Hitler renounces the Treaty of Versailles and begins to rearm openly.
Japan prepares to set up puppet state of North China.
Anglo-German Naval Agreement allows a new German navy of limited size.
OCTOBER: Mussolini invades Abyssinia.

1936

Rearmament is widespread in Europe.

Civil War in Spain (to 1939).

German troops enter Rhineland unopposed.

Japan and Germany sign Anti-Comintern Pact.

Rome–Berlin Axis established.

1937

JULY: Undeclared war breaks out between China and Japan – Japanese conquest of China begins.

Italy joins Anti-Comintern Pact.

1938

MARCH: *Anschluss* between Germany and Austria.

Hitler threatens to occupy Czechoslovakian Sudetenland.

SEPTEMBER: Munich Agreement forces Czechoslovakia to cede the Sudetenland to Germany and other territory to Hungary and Poland.

1939

MARCH: German troops occupy rest of Sudetenland.

MAY: Hitler and Mussolini form the Pact of Steel.

AUGUST: Anglo-Soviet talks break down.

AUGUST: Germany and the Soviet Union sign a Non-aggression Pact.

SEPTEMBER: German invasion of Poland prompts war with Britain and France. Poland divided between Germany and Soviet Union.

Soviet Union invades Finland.

1940

Japan announces idea of Greater East Asia Co-Prosperity Sphere and occupies northern Indo-China.

APRIL: Germany invades Denmark and Norway.

MAY: Germany invades the Netherlands, Belgium, Luxembourg and France.

JUNE: Italy joins European war on side of Germany. Fighting spreads to North Africa.

SEPTEMBER: Germany, Japan and Italy sign Tripartite Pact.

OCTOBER: Italy attacks Greece.

1941

APRIL: Germany invades Yugoslavia and Greece.

JUNE: Germany invades the Soviet Union.

JULY: Japan expands further into Indo-China.

US (and Netherlands) place embargo on sale of oil to Japan.

OCTOBER: Tojo becomes Prime Minister of Japan.

DECEMBER: Japanese attack US naval base at Pearl Harbor. USA and Britain declare war on Japan. Germany and Italy declare war on USA.

Glossary

alliance Formal agreement between two or more countries to help each other in times of war.

Allies, the Britain, France, the USA, Russia and their allies in World War I and World War II (when Russia was part of the Soviet Union).

annexed Took control of, usually by force.

armaments Weapons of all kinds.

Axis The alliance of Germany, Japan and Italy in World War II.

bankrupt Unable to pay one's debts.

cease-fire Agreement to halt a battle but not to end the war.

censorship Removing reports from the media that do not fit with the government's view.

civil war War within a single country.

colonies Countries or areas governed by another more powerful country.

communism The idea that wealth should be shared equally between all people and there should be no private property.

conscription Call-up; forcing people to join the army.

constitution Set of laws and customs by which a country is governed.

coup A sudden, illegal change of government.

demilitarized Free of military forces.

democracy Political system in which people are ruled by the law and by the people they elect to government.

dictator Unelected leader with absolute power.

diplomat Person who represents his or her state abroad.

empire A group of countries controlled by one ruler or government.

fascism An extreme right-wing political system that has one powerful leader and does not allow opposition.

garrison Base for soldiers.

Indo-China The modern countries of Vietnam, Cambodia and Laos.

inflation When money loses its value and prices rise.

isolationism The policy of not becoming involved in the affairs of other countries.

mutiny Refusal by members of the armed services to obey orders.

nationalism A feeling of pride in one's country, which sometimes means a person thinks it is better than any other.

Nazi Party The German fascist party led by Adolf Hitler.

pact Agreement.

pocket battleship Small battleship.

propaganda Information slanted to support only one point of view.

puppet state State set up and run by another.

putsch German word for a coup or attempted coup.

rearmament Building up the armed forces after a period of cutbacks.

Reichstag German parliament.

reparations Compensation payments.

republic A country that is governed by elected politicians. There is no king or queen.

revolution A complete and permanent change, for example in the government.

sanctions Orders to limit contact with a country, for example, refusing to trade with it, to try to make it obey international law.

Soviet Union Russia's communist empire – the Union of Soviet Socialist Republics.

stock market Market where stocks and shares (investments) are bought and sold.

Third Reich The Nazi regime in Germany, 1933–45. 'Reich' means empire or kingdom.

Totalitarianism A system of government in which only one political party has complete power and control.

treaty Formal written agreement between two or more countries.

ultimatum Final warning.

Further information

BOOKS

Nathan Anthony, Robert Gardner, *The Bombing of Pearl Harbor in American History* (Enslow, 2000)

Greg Lacey, Keith Shephard, *Germany 1918–1945* (John Murray, 1997)

John Malam, *1 September 1939: Hitler Invades Poland* (Cherrytree Books, 2002)

Stewart Ross, *Causes and Consequences: The Second World War* (Evans, 1995)

Sean Sheehan, *Germany and Japan Attack* (Hodder Wayland, 2000)

Richard Tames, *Pearl Harbor: The US Enters World War II* (Heinemann, 2001)

FOR OLDER STUDENTS

P. Calvocoressi, G. Wint & R. J. Pritchard, *Penguin History of the Second World War* (Penguin, 1999)

Courtney Browne, *Tojo: The Last Banzai* (Da Capo, 1998)

J.C. Fest, *Hitler*, (Penguin, 2002)

Martin Gilbert, *Descent into Barbarism: A History of the 20th Century* (HarperCollins, 1999)

R.J. Overy, *The Inter-war Crisis* 1919–1939 (Longman, 1994)

A.J.P. Taylor, *Origins of the Second World War* (Touchstone, 1995)

David Williamson, *War and Peace: International Relations 1914–1945* (Hodder and Stoughton Educational, 1994)

PLACES TO VISIT

World War II Memorial, Caen, France

Imperial War Museum, London

NOTE ON SOURCES

A source is information about the past. Sources can take many forms, from books, films and documents to physical objects and sound recordings.

There are two types of source, primary and secondary. Primary sources date from around the time you are studying; secondary sources, such as books like this, have been produced since that time. In general, primary sources are more accurate but contain much narrower information than secondary sources. Moreover, primary sources need handling with care.

Here are some guidelines to bear in mind when approaching a written or drawn primary source:

1. Who produced it (a politician, cartoonist, etc.?) and why? What was their motive? Were they trying to make a point?
2. When exactly was the source produced? What was going on at the time? Detail is key here, not just the year but sometimes even down to the exact time of day.
3. Might the source have been altered by an editor, censor, translator? (Possible change in translation is very important.)
4. Where was the source produced? Which country, town, region, etc?
5. Does the source tie in with other sources you have met, primary and secondary, or does it offer a new point of view?
6. Where has the source come from? Has it been selected by someone else (probably to prove a point – beware!) or did you find it through your own research? The only valid primary sources are those uncovered in genuine research.

Index